WISDOM
from the
ANCIENTS

WISDOM
from the
ANCIENTS

Edited by Simon Swain & Emilie Savage-Smith

BODLEIAN
LIBRARY
PUBLISHING

First published in 2023 by the Bodleian Library
Broad Street, Oxford OX1 3BG

www.bodleianshop.co.uk

ISBN 978 1 85124 614 4

Publisher: Samuel Fanous
Managing Editor: Susie Foster
Editor: Janet Phillips
Picture Editor: Leanda Shrimpton
Cover design by Dot Little at the Bodleian Library
Designed and typeset by Lucy Morton of illuminati
in 10½ on 14 Dante
Printed and bound in China by C&C Offset Printing Co., Ltd
on 120 gsm Chinese Baijin pure woodfree paper

British Library Catalogue in Publishing Data
A CIP record of this publication is available from the British Library

CONTENTS

Fill the vessel with perfume – that is to say,
Nurture your intellect with clarity,
discernment and wisdom.

SOCRATES

INTRODUCTION

It can be intriguing to pause – in the midst of our hectic, internet-driven lives of the twenty-first century – to consider what advice, what pieces of wisdom for leading a good life, were given to people living many hundreds of years ago in different parts of the globe. This volume presents over four hundred wise sayings, most of them incorporating fundamental truths about the human condition, that circulated widely among the Arabic-speaking communities of the twelfth and thirteenth centuries who lived (in modern terms) in the great expanse of territory from Spain to Central Asia that was ruled over by Muslim princes and dynasts.

One of the first things that a modern reader will notice about these wise sayings is that of the 404 assembled here, the vast majority (341) are attributed not to Arabic thinkers, but to six prominent figures from Greco-Roman antiquity. Only 63 sayings are attributed to Arabic scholars, distributed amongst sixteen different authors who lived from the seventh century to the late twelfth century CE. The dominance of advice from the Greco-Roman world demonstrates the very important role that the legacy of Greek antiquity played in the history and thinking of the medieval Arabic world.

A second feature of these pieces of wisdom that will draw the immediate attention of the modern reader is the fact that they are all attributed to men. More will be said below about the male voice that dominates such literature. Modern readers will also note that there is no racist stereotyping in these popular medieval sayings; nor are there any demeaning comments made regarding those of other religions.

Another notable characteristic is the predominance of advice relating to matters of health, as well as advice on what constitutes the best physician. This is not simply due to the source of these sayings for, in the world before modern treatments, disease was the most frightening occurrence in everyone's life, and advice on how to combat it was eagerly sought and followed.

In Greco-Roman antiquity and the medieval world of Byzantium and Islam, wisdom and advice were very often conveyed and remembered through concise and clever

sayings. The sayings offered here were written up by
Syrian physician Ibn Abī Uṣaybiʿah, the author of a highly
readable history of physicians and society that began with
the discovery of medicine and ran down to his own day in
the thirteenth century. Through these wise sayings, readers of today will find an entertaining yet reliable gateway
to medieval philosophy, medicine and culture – and in
particular a source of guidance for living their own lives
that in many ways is as authoritative and relevant now as
it was then. These are sayings to dip into, to read to your
friends, to be edified and above all to enjoy.

We have not attempted to document whether a
particular saying was actually said by the person named
or can be located in any surviving work of theirs. The
purpose of the present volume is to provide a twenty-
first-century reader with an idea of what wisdom and
advice on a range of topics of interest to the modern
world were circulating in the thirteenth century when
Ibn Abī Uṣaybiʿah wrote his book, and to see how people
of the medieval world confirmed their values through
wit as well as wisdom. Ibn Abī Uṣaybiʿah called his book
Best Accounts of the Classes of Physicians (ʿUyūn al-anbāʾ fī
ṭabaqāt al-aṭibbāʾ). He finished it shortly before he died
in about 1270 CE. It was intended to be a comprehensive
history of medical practice, and in it he surveyed the
lives and accomplishments of physicians from ancient

3

Greece and Rome, Persia, India and central Asia,
and across the southern Mediterranean shore over to
Spain, ending with the physicians of Egypt and Syria
who were his contemporaries. In the course of this
great work, he presents biographies of 432 individuals.
Many of these figures were revered as sages, whose
pronouncements were felt to embody the best of human
thought. For this reason, his book contains a large
number of their pithy sayings that were included both
to guide and to amuse.

Ibn Abī Uṣaybiʻah is in fact a nickname, and, as he
informs us, the nickname was also given to his grand-
father. It literally means 'the son (or descendant) of the
man with a little finger', and it suggests that an ancestor
of his had either a deformity or other distinctive feature
of his little finger. He came from a three-generation
family of physicians who had served various princes
and governors in Egypt and Syria, including the famous
Ayyubid ruler Saladin. He studied medicine under the
tutelage of his father and uncle, and with the leading
medical figures of the day, including al-Dakhwār (d. 1230
CE), the founder of a school in Syria devoted entirely
to the study of medicine. For each biography, Ibn Abī
Uṣaybiʻah compiled accounts of the person's achievements, followed by booklists of their writings and,
crucially, lists of their famous sayings. The majority of

the sayings are attributed to Greek figures who were as famous in medieval times as they are today: Pythagoras, Hippocrates, Socrates, Plato, Aristotle and Galen. They were part of the furniture of intellectual life and so authoritative that everyone wanted to abide by what they said. Ibn Abī Uṣaybiʿah did not, however, depreciate his own time, nor the extraordinary achievements of physicians, philosophers and scientists writing in Arabic. But wisdom needs age to embed it and that is why the ancient Greeks dominate, as you will see when you turn to the sayings, witticisms and riddles reproduced in the pages that follow. We hope that the resulting collection does not fall foul of the advice given by one Greek philosopher, Plato (d. 347 BCE), who is recorded as saying, with a certain dry humour, that 'Giving advice in excess casts many doubts upon the advice-giver.'

The lengthy history of physicians composed by Ibn Abī Uṣaybiʿah is preserved today in a surprisingly large number of handwritten manuscript copies – an indication of its popularity and importance. The Bodleian Library alone has eight copies,[1] the earliest transcribed in 1465 CE. In the eighteenth century some of these copies were used to prepare partial Latin translations of portions of the history, and more Latin translations of extracts followed in the nineteenth century, though these did not include the wise sayings or aphorisms.

APHORISMS

In English, such pithy bits of wisdom are often called 'aphorisms', a term derived from the Greek word used by the most famous physician of Greco-Roman antiquity, Hippocrates (d. *c.* 370 BCE), in his collection of medical advice called *Aphorisms*. The first of his aphorisms ('Life is short, the Art is long') has had a long and varied history, and it will indeed be found in the present collection of sayings, but here reflecting the Arabic version circulating in the thirteenth century CE: 'There is much to know, but life is short. Take the knowledge that you can achieve, from little to more' (see p. 22). Aphorisms reflect an oral tradition as well as a literary tradition, and hence our wise sayings often evolved or were modified as they passed from one generation or one culture to another.

In Arabic, from which all the following pieces of wisdom were translated, the most common term for a saying of this type was *ḥikmah* ('a piece of wisdom'). In ancient Greece, where aphorisms were also popular and a familiar part of educated culture, they were often called *gnōmai*, which gives us the modern word 'gnomic'. If anything, the aphorism was valued even more in the Islamic world – as is demonstrated by the present volume. The chattering classes of the medieval Islamic era, whatever their faith or their interest, were keen to demonstrate knowledge of their intellectual heroes.

Among the aphorisms and wise sayings recorded by
Ibn Abī Uṣaybiʿah, there are twenty short, cryptic sayings
that we would call 'riddles', for their meaning is not im-
mediately apparent and they require some explanation.
After each of these, Ibn Abī Uṣaybiʿah has inserted the
Arabic word *ay*, which means 'that is to say', and then
goes on to explain the meaning of the riddle. Of these
twenty gnomic riddles, six are attributed to Pythagoras
(d. *c.* 490 BCE) and fourteen to Socrates (d. 399 BCE), while
none are assigned to Arabic writers. Ancient Greek
culture loved riddles and regarded them as clever and
enjoyable ways of purveying wisdom about everyday
life.

The interest of the educated in being entertained and
instructed is not, of course, in any way restricted to the
distant past. Many later European thinkers, including
Blaise Pascal, René Descartes, Søren Kierkegaard and
Friedrich Nietzsche, composed examples of the art. The
poet W.H. Auden, in his anthology of modern aphorisms,
made a distinction between an aphorism and an epigram,
arguing that an epigram is valid only for a single in-
stance, while an aphorism expresses an idea that is either
universally true or true for every member of the group
to which it is addressed.[2]

In the first two decades of the twenty-first century
there has been a resurgence of interest in aphorisms

on the part of medical communities: the aphorism is as useful now for learning the medical arts as it was in the time of Hippocrates.[3]

WISDOM, MEDICINE & PHILOSOPHY

For Ibn Abī Uṣaybiʿah and his biographical subjects medicine had always been a bedfellow of philosophy, and in the medieval Islamic period one of the main words for physicians was also applied to philosophers, who often gave advice on how to endure the afflictions of the soul in its bodily abode. Hence, many of the authors of the sayings presented here are today thought of as philosophers rather than physicians. Ever-popular figures of the Greco-Roman world such as Plato and Socrates were known to Ibn Abī Uṣaybiʿah through Arabic translations made in the ninth and tenth centuries and reflect the respect given to the wisdom of antiquity that continued well past the thirteenth century. Today we may speak of 'the ancients' or 'the ancient world' to mean ancient Greece and Rome, and so could medieval writers in Arabic. And for Ibn Abī Uṣaybiʿah himself, the value of the wise sayings of 'the ancients' lay both in their ability to fill out gaps in the biographical material available to him and to offer readers the cream of practical wisdom from his heroes, who for him and his audience were models of the best physicians of bodies and souls.

MALE VIEWS

The voice throughout these sayings is distinctly male. Indeed, all the authors of the sayings were male, living and writing in a male world where they could imagine such wisdom being acted out. Attitudes and customs change over time and place, so that a few of the sayings in Ibn Abī Uṣaybiʿah's book are neither wise nor amusing for modern readers. Since the purpose of the present volume is to give both an insight into the wisdom of the past and guidance for living today, a handful of sayings from Ibn Abī Uṣaybiʿah's original work have been omitted. For example, it is consistent with this male-dominated world that misogyny can be found in some of the sayings, although the frequency of such comments is to us surprisingly low. Several misogynistic statements were attributed to Socrates (d. 399 BCE), the famous Greek philosopher of Athens, who supposedly said 'There is nothing more harmful than ignorance, and there is nothing worse than women.' Four other misogynistic comments were attributed to Socrates, who in one part of the Greek biographical tradition was said to have been bullied by his wife Xanthippe.

Apart from this, a few sayings make it apparent that, by the eighth and ninth centuries, sex with an elderly woman was considered medically harmful. For example,

to al-Ḥārith ibn Kaladah (seventh century), a physician
from Gondeshapur, there was attributed the saying:

> There are four things that will destroy the body:
> sexual relations on a full stomach, entering the bath
> after a heavy meal, eating dried salt meat and congress
> with an elderly woman.

Tayādhūq (also seventh century), an early physician
in Damascus, was assigned a similar statement, while
like sentiments were attributed to Bukhtīshūʿ ibn Jibrīl
(d. 870 CE), a Christian physician in Baghdad, and to
Yūḥanna ibn Māsawayh (d. 857 CE), another influential
physician in Baghdad.

There are in addition a number of sayings, including
one also attributed to al-Ḥārith ibn Kaladah, recom-
mending abstinence or moderation in sexual activities
in order to maintain good health. An example indicative
of misogynistic humour in medieval times is attributed
to Thābit ibn Qurrah al-Ḥarrānī (d. 901 CE), a Sabian
scholar living in Ḥarrān:

> There is nothing more harmful for the older man than
> to have a skilful cook and a beautiful young servant
> girl, since he will take an excess of food and become
> ill, and will engage in sexual intercourse to excess and
> become senile.

Slavery, a matter of great debate today, was as important an institution in medieval Islamic society as it had been in Greco-Roman antiquity, yet it is mentioned only once in the collection of sayings, in a statement attributed to Plato (d. 347 BCE):

> Never buy a slave who is governed by his passions, because he will have another master, nor a hot-tempered one who will resent your ownership, nor one with opinions, for he will employ ruse to deceive you.

Slaves were clearly not found entertaining or instructive.

A related area of concern today, ethnic stereotyping or racialist attitudes, is wholly absent in the sayings material. Neither race nor colour was an issue relevant to the best wisdom, and this reflects the multicultural, multiethnic nature of the society at the time. Stereotyping certainly went on, but the link between, for example, slavery and colour was not institutionalized as it became in early modern times. Ibn Abī Uṣaybiʿah lived in a world, like the Greco-Roman empire before it, where people of many different languages and cultures mixed and contributed at the highest levels. Prejudice and bias certainly existed and serious issues occurred, but the modern idea of the nation-state and the problems this entails were unknown.

Likewise, the three Abrahamic faiths of Judaism, Christianity and Islam were recognized, in accord with Islamic teaching, as worshipping the same deity; significantly, our wise sayings circulating in the thirteenth century do not touch on their differences.

It should be kept in mind that it was customary to formulate many sentences as 'he who does...' or 'a wise man should...' with the understanding that all persons, male and female, were intended to benefit – a convention maintained in many languages well into the twentieth century and in some places into the twenty-first century. Here the male voice speaks a wisdom for all.

In this collection, you can see that there was some adaptation of a saying as it moved through different peoples and times. For example, a reference to God in a Greek saying is presented in the Arabic version given by Ibn Abī Uṣaybiʿah with the insertion of the Muslim phrase 'may He be exalted', as in the saying 'Constant talk about God – may He be exalted – proves a man's incapacity to know him', which was attributed to the Greek philosopher Pythagoras (d. *c.* 490 BCE). In the collection assembled by Ibn Abī Uṣaybiʿah there was also considerable repetition of some earlier sayings by subsequent thinkers, with some later figures occasionally claiming the reworked aphorism as their own. Repetition, of course, is a sign of the value attached to a saying.

Ibn Abī Uṣaybiʿah presented these sayings in no particular order, nor under any subject headings. However, for the purposes of this volume, the English translations of these sayings have been grouped into topics (as listed in the table of contents), with the sayings presented in chronological order.

THE AUTHORS
OF THE SAYINGS

Pythagoras of Samos (d. *c.* 490 BCE), an ancient Greek philosopher known in later centuries as the founder of Pythagoreanism, a philosophy noteworthy for social regulation and enigmatic wisdom.[4]

Hippocrates of Cos (d. *c.* 370 BCE), the most famous physician of Greco-Roman antiquity, and author (with others) of the first treatises of medicine in the Greek tradition.[5]

Socrates (d. 399 BCE), the teacher of Plato and protagonist of his dialogues, who famously wrote nothing himself.[6]

Plato (*c.* 427–347 BCE), the most famous Greek philosopher, born in Athens.[7]

Aristotle (d. 322 BCE), the most distinguished of Plato's students, founder of the Peripatetic school of philosophy and the Aristotelian tradition of philosophy and logic.[8]

Galen of Pergamon (d. *c.* 200 CE), the most authoritative physician of the Roman era, with strong philosophical interests and an enormous influence on later medicine.[9]

al-Ḥārith ibn Kaladah (seventh century CE), an early Arabic-speaking physician who is said to have come from the Persian-speaking area of Gondeshapur.[10]

Tayādhūq (seventh century CE?), an early physician at the Umayyad court, known for his aphorisms and pithy sayings. The spelling of the name suggests a Greek origin, possibly Theodokos.[11]

Ibn Abjar al-Kinānī (seventh–early eighth centuries CE), a convert to Islam who is reported to have studied at the medical school in Alexandria and to have been physician to the Umayyad caliph ʿUmar ibn ʿAbd al-ʿAzīz (r. 717–720).[12]

Bukhtīshūʿ ibn Jibrīl (d. 870 CE), a Nestorian Christian physician at the Abbasid court in Baghdad. He was notable for having acquired greater wealth than any other physician of his time.[13]

ʿAlī ibn Rabban al-Ṭabarī (d. 855 CE) was born and raised in Tabaristan; after converting to Islam he became an influential figure at the court of the caliph and composed an important treatise on the art of medicine.[14]

Yūḥannā ibn Māsawayh (d. 857 CE), an influential physician in Baghdad and author of many treatises.[15]

al-Kindī, Yaʿqūb ibn Isḥāq (d. c. 870 CE), a very important philosopher and physician, known as 'the philosopher of the Arabs'.[16]

Ḥunayn ibn Isḥāq (d. c. 873 CE), a Christian physician working in Baghdad who was the major translator of Greek and Syriac treatises into Arabic.[17]

Thābit ibn Qurrah al-Ḥarrānī (d. 901 CE), a Sabian scholar and mathematician who lived in Ḥarrān.[18]

Isḥāq ibn Ḥunayn (d. c. 910 CE), translator of Greek philosophical texts and author of an early *History of Physicians*.[19]

al-Rāzī, Abū Bakr Muḥammad ibn Zakariyyā (d. 925 CE), physician and philosopher, born and raised in al-Rayy, an important city of west-central Iran – hence his name al-Rāzī – or Rhazes, as he was known to Europeans.[20]

Abū Sahl al-Masīḥī (d. 1010 CE), a distinguished Christian scholar and physician, was reputed to have been the teacher of Ibn Sīnā (d. 1037 CE), known to Europeans as Avicenna.[21]

Ibn Hindū, Abū l-Faraj (d. 1032 CE), an important poet and scholar writing on a wide range of topics.[22]

Ibn Riḍwān (d. *c.* 1061 CE) was born and raised in Egypt; he served the caliph al-Ḥākim in Cairo as chief of physicians.[23]

Ibn al-Tilmīdh, Amīn al-Dawlah (d. 1165 CE), a Christian court physician and practitioner in the ʿAḍūdī hospital in Baghdad.[24]

Ibn al-Ṣāʾigh al-ʿAntarī (d. after 1180/81 CE), scholar, poet and physician, active in Iraq and notable for his regimens and treatment of patients.[25]

THE
COLLECTED
SAYINGS

THE VALUE OF
WISDOM &
EDUCATION

You learn in the measure you seek,
and you seek in the measure you learn.

Pythagoras

Once Pythagoras said to an old man
who wanted to learn and was ashamed to be seen
as a student: 'Are you ashamed of being better at
the end of your life than at the beginning?'

Pythagoras

How useful are the discussions about precious and
important matters! But if someone cannot take
part in them, let him listen to those who do.

Pythagoras

There is much to know, but life is short.
Take the knowledge that you can achieve,
from little to more.

Hippocrates

Without practical work there is no search for knowledge,
and without knowledge there is no search for practical
work. Diminishing the truth out of ignorance is
preferable to then rejecting it out of ascetic ideals.

Hippocrates

With regard to knowledge, I praise myself
for knowing that I do not know anything.

Hippocrates

Knowledge is the spirit, and practice the body.
Knowledge is the root, and practice the branches.
Knowledge engenders while practice is engendered.
If practice were to occupy the place of knowledge,
no knowledge would take the place of practice.

Hippocrates

Practice is subservient to knowledge,
for knowledge is an aim. Knowledge
guides while practice is led.

Hippocrates

If the ignorant would remain silent,
disagreement would disappear.

Socrates

Intellect is a gift; knowledge an acquisition.

Socrates

No wise man possesses true wisdom until
he subdues his bodily impulses.

Socrates

Wisdom begins with good character.

Socrates

Socrates was once asked
why the water of the sea is salty,
and he replied: 'Tell me what you will gain
knowing that, and I will tell you why.'

Socrates

An ignorant man is someone who stumbles twice.

Socrates

Do not exceed the limits of the pan-scale
– that is to say,
Do not transgress the limits of truth.

Socrates

Wisdom is wealth that neither disappears nor dwindles.

Socrates

Search for three paths, but if you do
not find them, content yourself with sleeping
like one who has drowned – that is to say,
Seek knowledge of material and immaterial things,
and of that of immaterial nature that exists together
with material things. But allow yourself to neglect
that which is too difficult for you to know.

Socrates

A little education suffices the good soul (person),
but much education will not bear fruit in a bad
soul, because of the badness of its soil.

Socrates

Education is the most precious and incumbent
thing for young people, and the first benefit it
brings them is to prevent them from vile deeds.

Socrates

Experience is enough to educate, the vicissitudes
of time enough to admonish, and the morals of
those you frequent enough to instruct you.

Socrates

The tribulations of time suffice to teach a lesson.
Every day you will learn something new.

Socrates

Someone who gains experience increases his knowledge,
someone who believes increases his certainty. He who
is certain works hard, and whoever is eager to work
increases his power. But someone who is lazy becomes
weaker, and he who hesitates multiplies doubts.

Socrates

Fill the vessel with perfume – that is to say,
Nurture your intellect with clarity,
discernment and wisdom.

Socrates

If the wise man avoids people, search for him.
If he seeks them, avoid him.

Plato

He who seeks knowledge for its own sake will not
be worried by its inability to make him money,
but those who seek it for its profits will leave
their study for something that brings them gain
as soon as fortune abandons their family.

Plato

The goal of education is to give men
a sense of shame about themselves.

Plato

Aristotle asked Plato: 'When does a
man know that he has become a wise man?'
Plato replied: 'When he is not conceited in his opinions,
when his tasks are no longer a burden, and when
censure does not stir up anger nor praise pride.'

Plato

The advice reveals the nature of the adviser.

Plato

A wicked, learned man rejoices defaming the wise
men of the past and is grieved by those who live in his
time, because rather than wanting to learn from others
he is driven by his ambition for power. The good,
learned man is hurt when he loses the experience
of any of his peers, because his desire to increase
and enhance his knowledge through conversation is
greater than his desire for power and command.

Plato

An ignorant man once asked Plato:
'How did you learn so many things?'
Plato replied: 'Because I consume as much oil
(in the reading lamp) as you drink wine.'

Plato

Giving advice in excess casts many doubts
upon the advice-giver.

Plato

We love the truth and we love Plato, but when
they differ, truth is more deserving of our love.

Aristotle

A learned man recognizes an ignorant one
because he was once ignorant himself, but
an ignorant man does not recognize a learned
man because he has never learned.

Aristotle

I do not seek knowledge with the aspiration of reaching
its furthest point, nor aiming at possessing it all.
I only ask for that which cannot be ignored and that
which a sensible man cannot properly contradict.

Aristotle

Ignorance is the worst company.

Aristotle

Wisdom is the nobility of those without noble birth.

Aristotle

Since the ignorant is his own enemy,
how can anyone befriend him?

Aristotle

A happy man is someone who learns from others.

Aristotle

Aristotle once saw a young man who despised learning and told him: 'If you do not have the patience for the toils of learning, you will have to bear with patience the miseries of ignorance.'

Aristotle

After answering a question by one of his students, Aristotle asked; 'Have you understood?'
'Yes', answered the student.
But he insisted: 'You do not seem to have understood.'
'How can you know that?' said the student.
And Aristotle replied: 'I do not see you happy, and happiness is a sign of understanding.'

Aristotle

Experience is enough to acquire education, and the vicissitudes of time suffice to learn your lessons.

Aristotle

He who has tasted the sweetness of an action bears
patiently the bitterness of its pursuit. He who has seen
the utility of knowledge will seek to increase it.

Aristotle

When one of the students of Aristotle
vilified another student, Aristotle asked:
'Do you want us to accept what you have said
about him if we accept what he said about you?'
'No', he replied.
And Aristotle said: 'Refrain from
doing evil and it will evade you.'

Aristotle

One does not deserve blame for not answering a
question until it becomes clear that it has been asked
properly. A good question leads to a good answer.

Aristotle

The pen is the physician of logic.

Galen

Knowledge is useless if you don't understand it
– and understanding is also useless
unless you do something with it.

Galen

If a youth is greedy and utterly shameless,
there can be no expectation of him reforming.
If he is greedy and not shameless, one should not despair
of reforming him, but even if he receives an education
it cannot be presumed he will become a decent person.

Galen

The night is the erudite man's day.

Ḥunayn ibn Isḥāq

The intelligent person believes that there is knowledge
beyond the knowledge he has, and so he always humbles
himself to that additional knowledge. The ignorant
person believes that he has reached the summit,
and for this reason he is detested by the people.

al-Kindī

Frequent reading of scholarly books, and understanding
the secrets therein, is beneficial to every serious scholar.

al-Rāzī

With two glasses I spent my lifetime
and on them I always relied:
A glass filled with ink
and a glass filled with wine.
With one I established my wisdom
and with the other I removed
the worries of my breast.

Ibn al-Tilmīdh

Knowledge is an increase for an astute man and
a shortcoming for a stupid and frivolous man.
Just as the day gives more light to people's
eyes but covers the eyes of bats.

Ibn al-Tilmīdh

Whoever would like his name to be praised
then let him be much concerned with his knowledge.

Ibn al-Ṣāʾigh al-ʿAntarī

My son, seek learning, for if you gain nothing else in
this world you will at least be free of those who would
enslave you, whether by truth or by falsehood.

Ibn al-Ṣāʾigh al-ʿAntarī

The man of knowledge who is destitute
is more noble than an ignorant person
who is well provided for.

Ibn al-Ṣāʾigh al-ʿAntarī

The ignorant person seeks wealth, while
the person of knowledge seeks perfection.

Ibn al-Ṣāʾigh al-ʿAntarī

Wisdom is the nobility of those without noble ancestry.

Ibn al-Ṣāʾigh al-ʿAntarī

The ignorant person is a slave who cannot be
emancipated from bondage except through knowledge.

Ibn al-Ṣāʾigh al-ʿAntarī

The ignorant person is drunk and will not
sober up except through knowledge.

Ibn al-Ṣāʾigh al-ʿAntarī

Wisdom is the nourishment and adornment
of the soul. Wealth is the nourishment and
adornment of the body. When they both come
together in a person his imperfection ceases, his
perfection is complete, and his mind is at ease.

Ibn al-Ṣāʾigh al-ʿAntarī

Education adorns a person more than his
lineage, and has priority over his nobility, and
protects his honour more than his wealth, and
exalts his memory more than his beauty.

Ibn al-Ṣāʾigh al-ʿAntarī

RELIGION
& GOD

This world, albeit loved tenderly, is but a passing glance.

Verse in Arabic metre attributed to Socrates

Do not wear ring-stones with images of angels
– that is to say,
Do not reveal your religion
nor disclose the divine secrets to the ignorant.

Pythagoras

Whenever you seek to do something,
begin by praying to your Lord for success.

Pythagoras

Constant talk about God – may He be exalted –
proves a man's incapacity to know Him.

Pythagoras

The friend of God Almighty is the one who does
not abandon himself to his impure thoughts.

Pythagoras

Believe that God's fear is based on compassion.

Pythagoras

Reflection is especially suited to God, because the love
of reflection is bound to the love of God. Whoever loves
God – may He be exalted – inspires love for Him with
his actions. In so doing he becomes closer to God, and
those who are close to God are saved and succeed.

Pythagoras

Be content with your provision, do not be obstinate
and you will come close to God Almighty,
because God – may He be praised – does not need
anything, and whenever you need something
you move away from Him. Run away from evil,
flee from sins, and seek praiseworthy goals.

Hippocrates

It is a matter of wonder to those aware of
the temporality of the world how it distracts
them from that which is eternal.

Socrates

At the moment of death, do not be like an ant
– which is to say, Do not hoard the treasures of the senses
when you need to secure the salvation of your soul.

Socrates

When I search for the cause of life,
I find death, and precisely when I find death,
I know how I have to live – that is to say,
Whoever wants to live a godly life must mortify
his body in respect of all sensual acts in so far
as he has been endowed with strength. Only
then will he be able to live the true life.

Socrates

Nine is not more perfect than one – which is to say, the number ten is a compound number, being larger than nine, and the number nine is perfected becoming ten only by adding one. Similarly, the nine virtues are completed and perfected only through the fear, love, and observance of God, the Mighty and the Glorious.

(The nine virtues, according to Aristotle, are justice, courage, self-control, magnificence, magnanimity, liberality, gentleness, practical wisdom and speculative wisdom.)

Socrates

Justice is God's scale on earth, may He be exalted. With it, He takes from the powerful to the weak, to the truthful from the false. Whoever alters the balance that God has set for His subjects in His scale behaves with the utmost ignorance and makes the most fundamental error towards Him.

Aristotle

Enjoin yourself to uphold the law, because
in it resides the perfection of the pious.

Aristotle

Do not oppose those who are in the path of truth,
do not fight those who adhere to religion.

Aristotle

Let religion take the place of your king
and he who opposes religion will be his enemy.
Never reprove or abase those who uphold the law.
Take lessons from those who have passed
and do not be a bad example for
those who are to come.

Aristotle

Subdue the licentious, and you will improve
your religion and that of your people.

Aristotle

Do not accept anything from those who swear
falsely, for that turns the land into a wasteland.

al-Kindī

If a person during part of his day has an occupation
through which his body is kept in good shape and for
which people praise him and with which he earns a
sufficient amount, it is best he spend the remainder
of each day devoted to submission to God. And the
best form of submission is the contemplation of the
kingdom of God and praising its Ruler, may He be
glorified. Whoever has been provided for in that way
will be blessed in this world and the next, and will
have happiness and enjoy his reward in the hereafter.

Ibn Riḍwān

NATURE
& TIME

The world is an abode which at one time is for you,
and another time against you. If you are in control,
act properly; if you are controlled, yield yourself.

Pythagoras

This world is a prison for those who renounce it,
and a paradise for those who indulge in it.

Socrates

The world is like a fire burning on the highway:
Those who use it to light a torch and illuminate
their way will be free from its evil, but those
who sit there to claim exclusive possession
of it will be burned by its heat.

Socrates

Those who care about the world forfeit their souls.
Those who care about their souls renounce the world.

Socrates

Socrates said to a student: 'Never trust time,
for it is quick to betray those who rely on it.'

Socrates

He who is contented with time on one occasion
will be hurt by it on another.

Socrates

Do not try to work fast but to work well. People
will not ask about the time it took you to complete
your work, but only about its quality.

Plato

A man ought not to occupy his heart
with that which will abandon him, but
rather treasure that which remains.

Plato

On his deathbed, Plato was asked about the world,
and he said: 'I came to this world by compulsion,
and lived in it in perplexity; and here I am,
leaving it unwillingly, and not reckoning
anything but my ignorance of it.'

Plato

If you want freedom from want, then seek it through
contentment, because someone who does not
possess contentment will not be made free from
want by wealth, no matter how much there is.

Aristotle

There is no vainglory in that which perishes,
nor wealth in that which does not remain.

Aristotle

THE HUMAN CONDITION

If perfidy were innate to human nature,
trust would be impossible for everyone, and
if the means of life were equally divided,
greed would be pointless.

Hippocrates

IN GENERAL

If you do what you have to do in the way it should
be done, and (the result) is not as it should be, do
not change your actions as long as you see that
something from the original situation persists.

Hippocrates

Men have only one tongue and two ears
so that they might hear more than they talk.

Socrates

He who cares little about his losses
has a calm soul and a serene mind.

Socrates

You will not be perfect until your enemy trusts you.
What to say then, if you cannot
be trusted by your friend?

Socrates

Beware of those whom your heart loathes.

Socrates

Patience helps every undertaking.

Socrates

The one who hastens will often stumble.

Socrates

No boastful man can be praised, no choleric man
is happy, no honourable man is envious, no greedy
man is rich, no weary man lasts as a friend, no one
gains friendship with haste and then has regrets.

Aristotle

Better yourself and people will follow you.

Aristotle

Seek the wealth that does not perish,
the life that does not change,
the power that does not expire, and
permanence that does not vanish.

Aristotle

Do not be negligent, for negligence leads to remorse.

Aristotle

Bad manners destroy all that the ancestors built.

Aristotle

Learn from those who have preceded you,
remember what has passed, keep a healthy
life, and you will be successful.

Aristotle

Conceit is the belief of someone that he is what he
would love himself to be, whereas he is not.

Galen

Be gentle and you will succeed,
be kind and you will be noble.
But if you are conceited,
you will be despised.

Galen

The just man is capable of doing wrong yet does not.
The intelligent man has true knowledge of everything
that comes under (the category of) human knowledge.

Galen

The repose of the body is in minimum food, and the
repose of the soul is in having few sins. The repose
of the heart is in having few concerns, and the repose
of the tongue is in keeping speech to a minimum.

Thābit ibn Qurrah

THE MIND

Be fully awake when you think at all
times in your life, because the slumber of
thought shares the nature of death.

Pythagoras

As long as men remain in the sensible world,
they need to use their senses in the right
proportion, either a little or much.

Hippocrates

If the intellect of a man is not his dominant
trait, he will be defeated in most things.

Socrates

In time of war beware of employing bravery
but leaving your intellect aside. The intellect
sometimes suffices without need of courage, but
you will never see courage without intellect.

Plato

Everything has a special quality.
That of the mind is the ability to make good choices.

Aristotle

Let your writings be the best reading
and what you keep in your memory
be the best thing to write.

Aristotle

Sincerity is the basis of the affairs of all people.

Aristotle

THE SOUL

A free man does not let the tiniest part of
his soul go to waste on material pleasures.

Pythagoras

If you hear a lie let your soul bear it with patience.

Pythagoras

The soul comprises all things.
He who knows his soul knows everything.
He who does not know it knows nothing.

Socrates

Souls conform when their aspirations coincide, and
oppose each other when their desires diverge.

Socrates

Whoever is stingy with his soul is even more stingy
towards others; but generosity can be expected
from those who are generous with their souls.

Socrates

Everything bears its fruit, and having little brings
swift calm and goodness for the pure soul.

Socrates

When the love for this world inspires someone's soul,
he fills his heart with three feelings: (a sense of)
poverty that his wealth will never overcome,
hopes that his means will not fulfil, and
preoccupations that will never end.

Socrates

Sow with the black and harvest with the white
– which is to say, Sow with tears and reap with joy.

Socrates

Speak at night where there are no bats' nests –
which is to say, You ought to be in dialogue with
your soul in moments of solitude, when collecting
your thoughts, and prevent your soul from
concerning itself with material preoccupations.

Socrates

Cover all five windows to shed light on a place of illness –
which is to say, Shut your five senses off from wandering
in whatever is useless, in order to illuminate your soul.

Socrates

Empty the three parts of the basin of empty jugs
– which is to say, Free your heart of all the
pains that result from the three different
faculties of the soul (intellect, spiritedness and
appetite), which are the root of all evil.

Socrates

My soul aches for three things only: a rich man who
becomes poor, a powerful man who falls into disgrace,
and a wise man who is mocked by the ignorant.

Plato

Hope is a deceit for souls.

Plato

Let your main concern be the exercise of
your souls. As for the bodies, take care of
them in necessary measure, and abstain from
pleasures because they enslave the weak soul,
but they have no power over strong ones.

Aristotle

He who constantly thinks about death and
the afterlife improves his soul. And whoever
stains his soul is detested by his friends.

Aristotle

Just as disease and ugliness affect the body – disease
includes, for example, epilepsy and pleurisy, and
deformities such as hunchback, drooping of the
head and baldness – in the same way, disease
and ugliness affect the soul, whose disease is
anger and whose ugliness is ignorance.

Galen

Don't be prevented from doing good
just because your soul is inclined to do bad.

Galen

Wisdom is the lantern of the soul and,
when lacking, the soul is blind to the truth.

Ibn al-Ṣā'igh al-ʿAntarī

SELF-KNOWLEDGE

Think before acting.

Pythagoras

Be aware that things you ought to avoid might befall you.

Pythagoras

He who knows himself is never lost,
but how lost is he who does not know himself!

Socrates

Many a man wary of something
will find it to be his bane.

Socrates

Be aware that you follow the steps of those
who have already passed away, that you stand
in the place of those who are gone, and that
you will go back to where you came from.

Socrates

Socrates was asked:
'Why should an intelligent person ask for advice?'
He replied: 'The reason for it is a way to free someone's
opinion from emotion. We only seek advice
because we fear the consequences of emotions.'

Socrates

The good-doer is better than his good deeds,
the wrong-doer worse than his wrongs.

Socrates

Loyalty is the result of nobility.

Aristotle

In most people, reason succumbs to passion, because
they live with passion from childhood while reason
only comes with maturity. Their souls receive passions
like an old friend, but reason for them is a stranger.

Aristotle

Men are superior to animals for their ability to speak
and their intelligence. Someone who neither speaks nor
understands will be reduced to the animal condition.

Aristotle

It is possible for a person to improve his character
if he knows himself, for self-knowledge is the ultimate
wisdom. But because people naturally show an excessive
regard for themselves, they believe they are better than
they are. Thus some people suppose they are brave and
generous when they are not. Similarly, with regard to
intelligence, almost all men believe they are
superior, but people closest to this view
are the least in intelligence.

Galen

Worry is exhaustion of the heart,
while sorrow is a disease of the heart.
Clarifying this, Galen said:
'Sorrow is about something that happened;
worry about something that may happen.'

Galen

Sorrow is about what has gone,
worry is about something to come.
Watch out for it! For sorrow brings life to an end.
Don't you see that a living being in
sorrow will inevitably go to ruin?

Galen

And I see the defects of other people, without
seeing a defect in myself, even though it is closer to me.
Just as the eye reveals other faces, while its own face,
though close to it, is hidden from it.

Ibn al-Tilmīdh

SELF-IMPROVEMENT

It is better for a man not to err, but if he errs
nothing would help him more than acknowledging
his mistake and resolving not to repeat it.

Pythagoras

You should know the right moment to speak
and the right moment to remain silent.

Pythagoras

Nothing prevents a wise man from losing his temper,
but if anger seizes you let it be in a measured way.

Pythagoras

A wise man is not one who lets himself
be burdened to the full extent of his strength
and carries this burden patiently. The true wise
man lets himself be burdened with more than
nature allows him to bear and is still patient.

Pythagoras

The man who abstains from four things
will keep reproof away from him and from others.
These four things are: haste, stubbornness, vanity
and negligence. Because the fruit of haste is regret,
stubbornness bears perplexity, vanity hate,
and negligence contemptibleness.

Pythagoras

Do not stir the fire with a knife, if it is already hot
– which is to say, Do not use offensive words
when someone is already angered.

Pythagoras

Pythagoras used to sit in his chair and offer
seven pieces of advice: (1) Set up balances
and know their weights; (2) avoid mistakes
and you will always be blameless; (3) do not
kindle the fire where you see a cutting knife;
(4) restrain your passions and you will preserve
your health; (5) act righteously and you will be
surrounded by love; (6) manage your time as
if you were someone who might be appointed
and then dismissed; (7) do not accustom your
bodies and souls to an easy life or you will
lose them if you have to endure hard times.

Pythagoras

Help the carrier to transport his burden,
not to lay it down – which is to say,
No one should neglect his own duties
concerning virtue and obedience.

Pythagoras

Beware of being involved in anything
reprehensible, alone or in company, and be more
ashamed of yourself than of anyone else.

Pythagoras

Do not defile your tongue with calumnies,
nor expose your ears to them.

Pythagoras

He who possesses something has power over it,
but whoever wants to be free does not covet
that which he does not have, but rather he
flees from it lest he become its slave.

Hippocrates

Someone ungrateful for what has been bestowed
upon him is unlikely to improve his wellbeing.

Socrates

Do not give any thought
to someone who has no shame.

Socrates

Do not eat black-tailed animals
– which is to say, Beware of sin.

Socrates

He who wants to annihilate his passions
should only crave what he can attain.

Socrates

If you speak to someone more knowledgeable than you,
hold back your opinions and don't bother him with
verbiage. If you address someone less knowledgeable,
make your speech simple so that he may grasp by the
end what he has failed to understand at the start.

Plato

If your arguments prevail in a discussion with
an honourable man, he will show you honour
and invest you with dignity. If your arguments
succeed against a vile man, he will take you as
his enemy and seek to use them against you.

Plato

Men ought to look at their faces in the mirror.
If beautiful, they will detest spoiling their
beauty with wicked acts. If ugly, they will
abhor the idea of adding more ugliness.

Plato

If you give excessive advice, employ the pleasant
flattery used by people who deceive. Do not let yourself
be persuaded by your superiority over your peers or
else the fruits of your superiority will be spoiled.

Plato

Do not put too much onto the company of those
who collect people's faults, for they will extract
information from you about your failings and will tell
them to others as they have told you about others.

Plato

Do not waste your life on useless things, nor spend your
money on anything immoral, nor devote your efforts
to undemanding aims, nor occupy your mind with
wrongful thoughts, for you ought to protect what you
have and your good fortune, especially at that time of
life when everything is profitable. If you need to occupy
your soul with pleasures, let them be the conversation
with learned men and the study of books of wisdom.

Aristotle

Be merciful and compassionate,
and do not let your mercy and your compassion
fail those who deserve to be rewarded and
have improved themselves with education.

Aristotle

A concise speech encloses hidden meanings.

Aristotle

Silence is better than being inarticulate.

Aristotle

Hasty speech always leads to mistakes.

Aristotle

People hate the life of those excessive in reproof.

Aristotle

An honest way of life reduces examples of disgrace.

Aristotle

Pleasing all people is an impossible goal,
but do not worry about the anger of those
who are pleased with tyranny.

Aristotle

A man might be prepared to stop thinking
he is the smartest person in the world if he could
trust somebody to scrutinize every little thing
he does every single day and then inform him of
the correct and incorrect things he had done.
This would lead him to do what is fair
and avoid what is foul.

Galen

VICES & VIRTUES

Nothing is more righteous for a man
than doing what he has to do and
not what he wants to do.

Pythagoras

It is difficult for men to be free when the force of habit
drags them towards reprehensible and sinful actions.

Pythagoras

If you know a man personally and you find that
he is not good enough to be a righteous and loyal
friend, beware of making him your enemy.

Pythagoras

A man of good character covers the faults of others.
The man of bad character corrupts their virtue.

Socrates

Those who keep someone's secret without
being asked to do so are worthy of gratitude.
If they are asked to do it, it is a duty.

Socrates

Though keeping a secret may be a burden to you,
it will be a heavier burden to others.

Socrates

The man of good morals lives a pleasant life,
his well-being lasts, and people love him without fail.
Someone of bad character lives a miserable life,
hatred of him endures, and people shun him.

Socrates

One ought to know that there is
no time of the year without spring – which is to say,
Nothing prevents you from acquiring virtue at any time.

Socrates

Acquire twelve things with twelve things –
which is to say, Acquire virtues through the twelve
parts of the body whereby one attains either piety
or sin. They are: the eyes, the ears, the nostrils, the
tongue, the hands, the legs and the sexual organs.
Also: acquire in twelve months the various laudable
things that bring a man to perfection in this world
in respect of his self-management and knowledge.

Socrates

Whoever aligns the nobility of his origins with the
nobility of his soul does right for himself and may
truly claim his virtue. Whoever neglects his soul
by simply relying on the nobility of his ancestors
disavows them and does not deserve to be given
preference over anyone because of them.

Plato

A man is not fully magnanimous until
he is a sincere friend of those who oppose him.

Plato

In harsh times, virtues are not in demand and become
harmful, but vices are a requested and useful commodity,
and the fear of the wealthy is worse than that of the poor.

Plato

A man with good character is
he who endures those with a bad one.

Plato

The most noble people are those ennobled by their
virtues, not those who use their virtues to be honoured.
For if the virtues of a man are of his very essence, they
ennoble him. If they are accidental, he might use them
to be honoured but they do not make him a noble man.

Plato

Most virtues have a bitter inception and
sweet consequences, whilst most vices have a
sweet inception but bitter consequences.

Plato

Someone asked Plato: 'Who is safe
from vice and dishonourable deeds?' He replied:
'He who lets his intellect be his guardian, his
awareness his vizier, good advice his reins,
forbearance his commander, adherence to
devotion his assistant, fear of God his companion,
and awareness of death his intimate friend.'

Plato

Wicked men follow immoral people and avoid
the virtuous, just as flies are attracted to the
filthy parts of the body and leave the rest.

Plato

Do good to a noble man, and he will be encouraged
to reward you. Do good to a vile man, and
he will be encouraged to ask for more.

Plato

A man with a moderate sense of embarrassment
refrains from all that might bring him into
disrepute. But if it is excessive he will reject what
he needs, and if it falls short he will on most
occasions abandon the robes of decency.

Plato

He who, while on good terms, praises you
for qualities that you do not possess,
will vilify you when he is resentful
for vices that you do not have.

Plato

You should know that no one is free of fault or virtue.
Do not let the defects of a man prevent you from
requesting his help where he has no shortcomings;
nor let the many virtues of a man persuade you
to ask for his help when it comes to something for
which he has no means to help. But be also aware
that too much help from the wicked will be more
harmful for you than lack of help from the good.

Aristotle

Perfect your virtue by
abandoning that which does not concern you.

Aristotle

Fighting evil with evil is pain,
fighting evil with good is virtue.

Aristotle

Lying is an incurable disease for those afflicted by it.
Aristotle

Calumny fills hearts with hate.
He who confronts you (with slander) has in fact
calumniated you, but he who conveys slander
(about someone else) to you also slanders you.
Aristotle

Modesty renders a wealthy life perfect.
Aristotle

Ambition carries with it an inexpungible baseness.
Aristotle

Vileness destroys nobility
and exposes the soul to harm.
Aristotle

The tongue of the ignorant is the key
that opens the door to his destruction.

Aristotle

Calumny engenders nastiness.

Aristotle

Modesty is the fear of those who are ashamed of
a shortcoming that may occur in the presence
of someone who is more virtuous.

Galen

REPUTATION

The impression left by embellishments
and counterfeits does not last long.
Pythagoras

This world is not eternal, but
if you do good whenever it is possible,
you will be praised when you die,
leaving behind a good reputation.
Hippocrates

Good repute is better than wealth, which runs out,
whilst repute remains.
Socrates

Unless by saying 'I do not know'
I imply that I do know something,
I would say: 'I do not know.'

Socrates

A man of noble descent and poor morals
said to Socrates: 'Do you suffer disdain,
O Socrates, for the vileness of your origins?'
To which Socrates replied: 'Your noble descent
ends with you, mine starts with me.'

Socrates

A friend said to Socrates: 'What you said
to the people of the city was not well received.'
And Socrates replied: 'It does not concern me if it was
unacceptable, but I am concerned that it was right.'

Socrates

Plato was asked:
'What is the most profitable thing for men?'
He replied: 'To care for his own rectitude
more than for that of others.'

Plato

Seek in this life knowledge and wealth
and you will gain ascendancy over people,
for they are either nobles or commoners. The
nobles will value you for what you excel in,
the commoners for what you have.

Plato

Many a man is counted happy for a good fortune
that is actually a trial, and many are envied
for a condition that is in fact a malady.

Plato

During your life seek wisdom, wealth and
good deeds, because the nobles will like you for
the things you master, the commoners for what you
possess, and everybody for what you have done.

Plato

He who received praise after his death is in a better state
than someone who received criticism during his life.

Aristotle

Status grows through bestowing favours.

Aristotle

Grant pre-eminence to the pious, the virtuous and
the faithful, and in return you will be rewarded
with success and distinction in this world.

Aristotle

Authority comes with heavy burdens.

Aristotle

He who searches for the hidden vices of his friends
will never have any authority.

Aristotle

Seeking those who avoid you is dishonourable,
avoiding those who seek you shows lack of ambition.

Aristotle

Losing one's face by begging from people
is a lesser death.

Aristotle

SORROW

If adversity befalls you, be patient and, instead of
complaining, spare no effort to find a remedy.

Pythagoras

Someone said to Socrates:
'We have never seen you sad.' He replied:
'It is because I do not have anything the
loss of which would sadden me.'

Socrates

There are six kinds of persons
who are always filled with sorrow:
(1) the resentful, (2) the envious, (3) the nouveau
riche, (4) the rich man who fears poverty, (5) he who
craves a high status that he is unable to achieve,
and (6) he who frequents people of erudition and
good manners without being one of them.

Socrates

Someone tough in spirit does not succumb to misery.

Plato

Show fortitude when worry overcomes you,
for the worry and he who caused it will not last.

Ibn Hindū

Sorrow is the night of the heart and joy is its day.
To drink poison is easier than to
suffer oppressive thoughts.

Ibn al-Ṣāʾigh al-ʿAntarī

THE BODY & HEALTH

Do not neglect the health of your body:
You ought to eat, drink, practise sex
and exercise with moderation.

Pythagoras

GENERAL

Health is a light possession,
but those who lack it understand its might.

Hippocrates

In order to preserve health, one should not be too lazy
to exercise and should stop overeating and drinking.

Hippocrates

A man in bad physical shape as a result of illness,
even if he is into his fifties, does not give up and let his
body go to waste and ruin, but asks for his health to be
restored, even if he cannot be helped to regain it in full.
In the same way we ourselves must not stop improving
ourselves with regard to both health and virtue, even
if we cannot match the virtue of a true philosopher.

Galen

Do not eat until you are hungry; do not engage
in sexual relations if you feel reluctant; never
hold in your urine; and always remember that
the bath is a good servant but a bad master.

Tayādhūq

When you eat a meal during the day, there is
no harm in having a nap, but when you eat a meal
at night, do not go to bed without having gone for
a walk, even if it is no more than fifty paces.

Tayādhūq

Taking a nap during the day after eating
is better than swallowing a beneficial syrup.

Abū Sahl al-Masīḥī

A body free from defects is a healthy body in which
each of its parts maintains its inherent efficacy, by which
I mean it performs its special function as it should.

Ibn Riḍwān

FOOD, DRINK & WINE

We eat to live, not live to eat.

Hippocrates

When healthy, men can eat like beasts;
but if they fall ill, they should be
fed like birds in order to heal.

Hippocrates

Do not eat for the sake of eating.

Hippocrates

Wine is a friend for the body,
apples are friends for the soul and the spirit.

Hippocrates

Wine should be served to wise men,
(poisonous) hellebore to the stupid.

Hippocrates

Do not drink immoderately because it alters
your mind and impairs your discernment.

Aristotle

He who drinks without restraint is a lowlife.

Aristotle

When Aristotle saw a convalescent patient eating
excessively because he believed that this would make
him stronger, he said: 'The increase of strength
does not depend on the amount of food that the
body receives, but on the amount that it accepts.'

Aristotle

Of wine:
The finer the flavour, the more enjoyable.
The purer, the more wholesome. The sweeter,
the more stimulating to desire. Do not drink
it neat, for it will leave you with a headache
and bring on an array of illnesses.

al-Ḥārith ibn Kaladah

Eating apples restores the soul.

Yūhannā ibn Māsawayh

You should have food that is new and wine that is old.

Yūhannā ibn Māsawayh

To drink on an empty stomach is harmful.
To eat on a full stomach is more harmful still.

Bukhtīshū' ibn Jibrīl

It is better to eat a small quantity of something harmful
than a large quantity of something beneficial.

Bukhtīshūʿ ibn Jibrīl

Wine in moderation is a friend to the spirit;
wine in excess is an enemy of the body.

Isḥāq ibn Ḥunayn

If the physician is able to treat a patient
using foodstuffs rather than medicines,
then he has been truly fortunate.

al-Rāzī

One glass quenches the flame of thirst,
A second helps to digest one's food,
The third helping of wine is for joy,
And one's mind is driven out
by adding another cup.

Ibn al-Tilmīdh

ILLNESSES & AFFLICTIONS

The heart's frailty within the human body is
like that of the eyes behind the eyelids.

Hippocrates

The heart suffers from two kinds of harm: sorrow
and anxiety. Sorrow affects him during sleep, and
anxiety during wakefulness. This is because anxiety
appears when someone reflects with fear about that
what is to come, which needs wakefulness. Sorrow,
however, does not involve any reflection, because
it only feeds on that which is past and finished.

Hippocrates

Illnesses befall people for four reasons:
a specific cause, a bad diet, mistakes
or the enmity of Satan.

Galen

On the stone of Galen's signet ring was inscribed:
'If a man hides his illness, it will be completely
impossible to find a cure for it.'

Galen

As the longitude and latitude of the fixed stars change,
so do the dispositions, temperaments
and habits of people.

al-Rāzī

Hot illnesses are more lethal than cold ones
due to the rapidity of the movement of fire.

al-Rāzī

MEDICINES

Treat each sick person with drugs from his own land,
because nature finds protection in what is familiar to it.

Hippocrates

Do not take medicines unless necessary,
because if you take them without need and
there is no disease to fight, your health will be
affected by them and a disease will appear.

Hippocrates

When Hippocrates was asked: 'Why does the body
become most agitated when someone drinks medicines?'
Hippocrates replied: 'For the same reason the house
becomes most full of dust when it is being swept.'

Hippocrates

A sick man gets relief from the breeze in his land,
just as a barren land is refreshed by the
moisture of dripping rain.

Galen

Avoid taking remedies while in good health, but if
some disease strikes, take something to repel it before
it has taken root and grown strong. The body may
be likened to the earth: care for it, and it will thrive,
but if you neglect it, it will go to rack and ruin.

al-Ḥārith ibn Kaladah

Avoid taking medicine if you possibly can.
Drink it if you must, but it is likely to
do you as much harm as good.

al-Ḥārith ibn Kaladah

Refrain from taking medicine
as long as your body can bear the illness.

Ibn Abjar al-Kinānī

In keeping with the differences
between the latitudes of cities, there are
differences in dispositions, temperaments, habits,
and the nature of medicines and foodstuffs, so that
a drug of the second degree may be in the fourth,
and vice versa.

al-Rāzī

Life is too short to understand the effect of every
plant growing on earth, so use the most well known
for which there is a consensus and avoid the unusual.
Confine yourself to what you have tried and tested.

al-Rāzī

THE ART OF MEDICINE

Carved on the stone of Hippocrates' ring:
'I have more hope in a sick person with an appetite
than in a healthy man without one.'

Hippocrates

Medicine encompasses theory and experience.

Hippocrates

Every disease of known origin has a cure.

Hippocrates

Combating passions is easier than treating diseases.

Hippocrates

Saving (patients) from severe diseases is a hard task.

Hippocrates

Once Hippocrates visited a patient and said:
'We are three altogether: the disease, you and I.
If you cooperate and accept all that I say, we will
become two, the disease will be left alone and
we will be strong against it; because when two
join forces against one, they succeed.'

Hippocrates

There are five ways to treat the whole body:
the head by gargling, the stomach by vomiting,
the body with purgatives for the bowels, the parts
between the two skins (the epidermis and the
hypodermis) by sweating, and the insides and
the interior of the veins by bloodletting.

Hippocrates

Reducing harm is better than increasing benefit.

Hippocrates

Hippocrates said to one of his students:
'Let your best practice be your love for the people,
and your preoccupation with knowing their problems
and conditions, and for doing them good.'

Hippocrates

Giving to the sick something that he desires
is more beneficial than forcing on him what he dislikes.

Hippocrates

The intelligent man should talk to the ignorant
like the physician talks to the sick.

Socrates

Upon seeing an ignorant physician, Plato exclaimed:
'This one encourages and arouses death.'

Plato

There is more hope for a sick man with an appetite
than for a healthy man without one.

Galen

Nature is like a plaintiff and illness is the litigant.
The symptoms are like the witnesses, and the urine
flask and the pulse are the evidence. The critical day is
like the day of the judgement and the verdict, and the
patient is the attorney, while the physician is the judge.

Galen

A statue cannot be made from any stone,
and it is not every dog that is good for fighting lions.
In the same way we will find that not everybody
is receptive to (practising) the art of medicine,
but we need someone whose body and
soul are well suited to the purpose.

Galen

The ignorant physician encourages death.

ʿAlī ibn Rabban al-Ṭabarī

Let the physician be mindful of God, exalted is He,
and let him not take risks, for there is nothing that will
compensate for the loss of human life.

al-Kindī

Just as (the physician) likes to be told that he
was the cause of the patient's well-being and
his cure, let him fear lest he be told that he was
the cause of his destruction and his death.

al-Kindī

The physician, even though he has his doubts,
must always make the patient believe that
he will recover, for the state of the body
is linked to the state of the mind.

al-Rāzī

Certainty in medicine is an unattainable goal –
and the treatment of patients according to what
is written in books, without the skilful physician
using his own judgement, is fraught with danger.

al-Rāzī

Physicians who are illiterate and tradition-bound,
those who are young and careless, and those
who are debauched – they are lethal.

al-Rāzī

Whoever does not concern himself with the
natural and philosophical sciences and the
canons of logic, but inclines towards worldly
pleasures – be suspicious of his knowledge,
particularly with regard to the art of medicine.

al-Rāzī

When convalescents crave a certain food which is
harmful to them the physician should manage the
situation in such a way as to replace that foodstuff
with something whose qualities are appropriate, and
not simply refuse the patients what they crave.

al-Rāzī

The student of medicine who studies with
many doctors runs the risk of falling into
the errors of each one of them.

al-Rāzī

The patient should confine himself to a
single trustworthy physician as he will
err but little and often be correct.

al-Rāzī

It is incumbent upon the physician to not neglect
to question the patient about all the internal and
external symptoms caused by his illness, for then
he can come to a much better conclusion.

al-Rāzī

When the physician confines himself to
experience without also using sound reasoning
and the study of books, he will fail.

al-Rāzī

Confidence should not be placed in the excellence
of the medical care provided by a physician until he
(the physician) reaches maturity and gains experience.

al-Rāzī

The physician's behaviour should be balanced –
neither completely concerned with worldly matters,
nor completely absorbed in otherworldly matters
– and so be positioned between hope and fear.

al-Rāzī

Let yourself be guided by what is subject to
the consensus of the physicians, attested by
sound reasoning, and supported by experience,
but do not do so if that is not the case.

al-Rāzī

When you are summoned to a patient,
give the patient something that will not harm him
until you determine his illness. Only at that point
should you treat it. Identifying the disease means
you must first determine from which humour it has
arisen and then, after that, the part of the body in
which it is located. At that point, you may treat it.

Ibn Riḍwān

The physician, according to Hippocrates,
should encompass seven qualities:
(1) He should have excellent moral character, a healthy
body, a keen intelligence and a pleasing appearance,
while also being prudent, possessing an excellent
memory and having a good disposition. (2) He should
be well-dressed, pleasant smelling and be clean in his
body and attire. (3) He should respect the confidences of
patients and not divulge anything about their illnesses.
(4) His desire to cure those who are ill should be greater
than his desire for any payment he might request. His
desire for treating the poor should be greater than his
desire to treat the rich. (5) He should be eager to teach
and do his utmost to benefit the people. (6) He should
be sound of heart, modest in appearance and truthful in
speech, while paying no attention to anything regarding
the women or the wealth that he sees in the houses of
the upper classes, let alone meddling with any of them.
(7) He should be trustworthy with regard to people's lives
and property, neither prescribing any lethal medicine nor
giving instructions regarding one, nor any drug causing
abortion, and he should provide treatment for his enemy
in no less correct a manner as he would treat his friend.

As summarized by Ibn Riḍwān

DEATH

When death struck Pythagoras' wife in
a foreign land, his friends offered their condolences
for her death, lamenting the fact of her dying abroad,
but he said: 'O friends! There is no difference
between dying at home or abroad, for the path
to the next world is the same from every land.'

Pythagoras

Death purges the world of the evil of the wicked.

Socrates

Despise death, for its bitterness resides in the fear of it.

Socrates

The people in this world pass away
like figures in a scroll: when part of it
is spread out, part of it is rolled up.

Socrates

Sleep is a brief death. Death is a long sleep.

Socrates

Socrates was asked:
'What is the nearest thing?' – 'This world', he replied.
'And the furthest?' – 'Hope.'
'What is the most sociable thing?' – 'A congenial friend.'
'And the loneliest thing?' – 'Death.'

Socrates

He who cares about the material world and
attains what he craves will leave it for someone else.
If he does not attain it, he will die in distress.

Socrates

He who dies has few who may envy him.

Aristotle

He who loves the world immoderately dies poor.
The contented man dies rich.

Aristotle

Death comes from four causes:
(1) natural, that is from old age; (2) disease;
(3) desire, for example suicide or yielding to death;
and (4) sudden death, which is a total surprise.

Galen

When someone asked Galen
when a man must die, he replied,
'When he cannot tell what harms him
from what helps him.'

Galen

SOCIETY

Do not step over the balance
– which is to say, Avoid excess.

Pythagoras

Pythagoras once saw a man wearing splendid
clothes who suffered from a speech impediment.
Pythagoras told him: 'Either you use a language
that matches the quality of your clothes or
wear clothes that match your language.'

Pythagoras

Hippocrates was asked: 'What is the best life?'
He replied: 'Poverty in safety
is better than riches in fear.'

Hippocrates

A man should behave in his worldly existence
like the guest in a banquet who takes a cup only
when he is offered one and, if the cup passes him over,
does not stare at it or reach for it. This is how he should
conduct himself with people, wealth and descendants.

Hippocrates

He who guards his secret
conceals his affairs from the people.

Socrates

Do not correct the mistakes of those who live in error.
They will profit from your knowledge
and still consider you an enemy.

Socrates

Praise those you love to whomever you
encounter, for love begins with praise, just as
enmity begins with dispraise.

Socrates

If you are given a position of authority, keep bad people
far from you or you will be blamed for all their faults.

Socrates

Treat your parents as you want your sons to treat you.

Socrates

The silent man will be regarded as inarticulate,
but he will be safe. The one who speaks will be
considered interfering, and will regret it.

Socrates

Keep the secrets of others
as you wish others to keep your own secrets.
Socrates

Heal wrath with silence.
Socrates

If you need to ask someone to keep
your secret, do not confide it to him.
Socrates

Do not share what you have in your soul
with everyone. How disgraceful it is that people
conceal their precious things at home whilst
they expose the content of their hearts.
Socrates

May the ingratitude of the ungrateful
never turn you away from doing good deeds.

Socrates

Do not raise the crown only to dishonour it –
which is to say, Do not shun virtuous customs,
for they surround all nations just as the band
of the crown surrounds the head.

Socrates

Do not associate with evil-doers. The only benefit
you will receive from them is that they leave you alone.

Plato

Do not judge anyone by the status that circumstances
have given to them, but by their real worth,
which is the rank granted to them by nature.

Plato

Do not befriend the wicked man
or your nature will become imbued with
his evil without you even being aware of it.

Plato

The decisive man ought to prepare himself for business
to the extent demanded by reason, but should not rely on
those factors that fall beyond his reach and he hopes to
achieve, or on those which are the result of habit. These
factors are not in his power but rather the outcome of
coincidences on which his decisiveness should not trust.

Plato

Plato was once asked:
'What should one be wary of?'
He replied: 'Of the powerful enemy,
the troublesome friend
and the wrathful lord.'

Plato

SOCIETY

The intelligent man ought to acquire only that
which adds to his qualities, and only serve
those who are close to him in character.

Plato

Aristotle was once asked:
'What is that which you should not say
even it if is true?' He replied: 'You should
never praise yourself.'

Aristotle

The intelligent person should choose a manner of
dress such that neither the commoners envy him
for it nor the elite look down on him for it.

Ibn al-Tilmīdh

When you are envied you are an eyesore in people's
eyes, so apply to them the kohl (eye salve) of humility.

Ibn al-Tilmīdh

Be rich if you can, or else be wise;
all things but these two are useless.

Ibn al-Ṣāʾigh al-ʿAntarī

He who keeps silent acquires respect,
which hides his bad qualities from people.

Ibn al-Ṣāʾigh al-ʿAntarī

POLITICS & POWER

Many enemies mean little peace.

Pythagoras

Do not walk by the dens of the lions – which is to say,
Do not follow the ideas of the rebellious.

Pythagoras

Swallows do not live in houses – which is to say,
Do not be like those arrogant and garrulous
men who cannot control their own tongues.

Pythagoras

The worst thing for your enemy
is for him not to realize you
consider him an enemy.

Pythagoras

Whoever befriends the ruler should not worry
about his severity, just as the pearl diver does
not worry about the salt in the sea water.

Hippocrates

The mightiest king
is the one who subdues his passions.

Socrates

When Plato was asked who was the most reliable man
to entrust with the regulation of the city he replied:
'The one who regulates himself in a virtuous way.'

Plato

A king is like a powerful river from which
smaller rivers derive. If sweet-watered they will have
sweet water, if salty they will be salty as well.

Plato

Do not underestimate your enemy
or adversity will overwhelm you the more so
in proportion to the way you assess him.

Plato

The tyrant is at ease so long as he respects the principles
of civilization and the foundations of religious law.
But if he takes aim at them, the Master of the World
will set against him and he will be annihilated.

Plato

The best kings are remembered as just rulers and
their virtues taken as a model by their successors.

Plato

When your enemy falls under your power,
he is no longer one of your enemies but a subordinate.

Plato

Authority is a necessity in this world
due to the overwhelming weakness of its people.

Plato

You ought to be more fearful about the way you
treat your enemy than about the way he treats you.

Plato

Men's passions are roused in the same degree
as the passions and desires of their king.

Plato

Protect the laws that will protect you.

Plato

Necessity opens the door to stratagems.

Aristotle

Treat your weakest enemies as if they were stronger
than you, and inspect your army like someone who has
suffered a calamity and is in need of their protection.

Aristotle

Know that nothing is more beneficial for people
than their rulers, but only if they are righteous.
There is nothing worse for them and their souls
than a corrupt one, because the ruler is to his subjects
as the soul is to its body, which cannot live without it.

Aristotle

Treat your subjects kindly, like someone whose kingdom
has been violated and whose enemies are many.

Aristotle

Do not expect safety for yourself until the people are
safe from your injustice, and do not punish anyone
for something that you would allow for yourself.

Aristotle

He who disputes with the ruler
dies before his day.

Aristotle

People desire the demise of those
who behave tyrannically with them.

Aristotle

A king who disputes with the common people
dishonours himself.

Aristotle

Death is the noblest end for a king
who had driven himself to ignominy.

Aristotle

The ruler ought not to take money or goods from
the common people, but rather adopt them and
welcome them as friends. He should not desire from
them honour other than that which he deserves for
his good deeds and his virtuous administration.

Aristotle

Giving advice to Alexander the Great, Aristotle wrote:
'The corrupt are easily led by fear; the honest by shame.
You should discriminate between both groups.
With the former be rough and ruthless,
with the latter gracious and beneficent.'

Aristotle

He also told him: 'Let your anger be moderate,
neither merciless nor pusillanimous. The former
is proper to beasts, the latter proper to children.'

Aristotle

He also wrote to him: 'The deeds that bring honour to
kings are three: virtuous laws, celebrated conquests,
and the cultivation brought to barren lands.'

Aristotle

He wrote once to Alexander:
'If God grants you the victory you want,
be merciful as He wishes.'

Aristotle

Do not despise an enemy who seems feeble,
even though he has little force or toughness:
The fly has the power to inflict a festering
wound, a power of which a lion falls short.

Ibn al-Tilmīdh

A man's power lies in wealth and knowledge;
poverty and ignorance have never reigned.

Ibn al-Ṣāʾigh al-ʿAntarī

LOVE, SEX & FRIENDSHIP

A man's most precious possession
is a sincere friend.

Socrates

Intelligent persons fall in love when they share their rational abilities, but love does not occur between idiots when they share their idiocy, because reason flows in an organized stream (of thought) which two people can share, while idiocy flows in a confused way and two people cannot coincide.

Hippocrates

Someone asked Hippocrates:
'How often should sexual intercourse be performed?'
And he replied: 'Once a year.'
'And if this cannot be achieved?' they said.
Hippocrates replied: 'Then once a month.'
'And if this is also impossible?' they asked.
To which Hippocrates replied: 'Then once a week.'
'And if this is not possible?' they insisted.
And Hippocrates said: 'It is his soul,
he may let it go whenever he wants.'

Hippocrates

Coitus consumes the water of life.

Hippocrates

The eyes of the lover are blind
to the defects of the beloved.

Plato

If you become the intimate friend of a man,
you should be the friend of his friend,
but not the enemy of his enemy.

Plato

The best things are the newest, except for friendships,
for the best of them are the oldest.

Aristotle

Passionate love is finding someone attractive
– as well as wanting them.

Galen

MONEY &
POSSESSIONS

Earn money by rightful means
and spend it accordingly.

Pythagoras

Do not crave worldly goods or lofty buildings.
Men die, but after their owner's death these
goods will remain so far as their natures allow.
Seek instead all that can be enjoyed and will
benefit you after the (final) departure.

Pythagoras

Money was mentioned in the presence of
Pythagoras and was praised. Pythagoras said:
'I do not have any need of that which fate gives,
miserliness preserves and generosity kills.'

Pythagoras

Having few people dependent
on oneself is a great fortune.

Hippocrates

He who seeks worldly things
will have a short life and many worries.
Socrates

Every possession implies servitude,
and someone who serves something
other than himself is not free.
Socrates

Socrates was once asked:
'What is a praiseworthy acquisition?'
He replied: 'Something that increases
in value against the outlay on it.'
Socrates

When calamity strikes,
those who live in ease are grieved by their wealth.

Socrates

Prefer legitimate poverty to forbidden wealth.

Socrates

The most virtuous way of life
is to make an honest profit
and control one's expenses.

Socrates

Every possession is a source of sorrow:
do not acquire sorrow.

Socrates

Have few possessions
and your misfortunes will be few.

Socrates

He who in wealth is not generous with his friends
will be abandoned by them in poverty.

Plato

Someone asked Plato: 'Why does a man
persevere in amassing wealth even in old age?'
He replied: 'Because he prefers to leave his wealth
to his enemies after his death, rather than needing
the help of his friends during his life.'

Plato

PLEASURES
& DESIRES

Pythagoras was once asked:
'What are the most pleasant things?'
He replied: 'All things that men desire.'

Pythagoras

Do not seek in anything that which satisfies your desires, but desire that which is desirable by itself.

Pythagoras

The most pleasurable things in this world are four: food, drink, sexual intercourse and listening (to music). Three of these pleasures – or that which is related to them – cannot be attained but with great effort and difficulty, and they are harmful when enjoyed in excess. But listening (to music), in dearth or in excess, is an undemanding and effortless pleasure.

Hippocrates

Hippocrates said to one of his students:
'If you do not want to succumb to your passions, covet only what you can attain.'

Hippocrates

When asked once about undesirable things,
Hippocrates remained silent. They asked him:
'Why do you not reply to that?'
And he said: 'Silence was my answer.'

Hippocrates

The best of everything is its middle point.

Socrates

When Socrates was asked:
'What is the most pleasurable thing?'
he replied: 'The benefits of education and
learning things that you did not know.'

Socrates

On being asked about lust, Galen said:
'A trial that can be expected not to last.'

Galen

Someone said to Galen: 'Why do you go to parties and places of entertainment?' 'So I can know (human) faculties and natures in every situation of sight and sound', Galen replied.

Galen

Listening to songs is like severe pleurisy because a person listens and becomes joyful and then spends of his money to excess and so is impoverished and becomes melancholic and falls ill and dies.

al-Kindī

*You should know the right moment to speak
and the right moment to remain silent.*

PYTHAGORAS

SOURCES

For the six writers from classical antiquity, two major sources were used by Ibn Abī Uṣaybiʿah.

Choice Wise Sayings and Fine Statements (Mukhtār al-ḥikam wa-maḥāsin al-kalim) is by al-Mubashshir ibn Fātik, an Egyptian historian and savant (*fl. c.* 1048 CE). This treatise, which combines biographical sketches of Greek sages with collections of their sayings, has had a modern printing as al-Mubashshir ibn Fātik, *Mukhtār al-ḥikam wa-maḥāsin al-kalim*, ed. ʿAbd al-Raḥmān Badawī (Madrid, 1958; Beirut, 1980).

A variant version of the treatise circulated in the Muslim West, and about 1250 it was translated into Spanish as *Bocados d'oro*, but without the author's name. This anonymous Spanish version was then translated into Latin and several European vernaculars including

French, Provençal and English. Following the invention of moveable-type printing, the vernacular versions were printed in large numbers, with the English text printed in 1477 by William Caxton as *Dictes and Sayenges of the Phylosophers*. For a modern printing of the English version, see Mubashshir ibn Fātik, *Dicts and Sayings of the Philosophers, the Translations made by Stephen Scrope, William Worcester, and an anonymous translator*, ed. Curt F. Buehler, Early English Text Society, no. 211 (London: Oxford University Press, 1941).

See also *Encyclopaedia of Islam*, 2nd edn, article 'al-Mubashshir b. Fātik' (F. Rosenthal); Dimitri Gutas, *Greek Wisdom Literature in Arabic Translation: A Study of the Graeco-Arabic Gnomologia* (New Haven CT, American Oriental Society 1975); and Dimitri Gutas, 'Classical Arabic Wisdom Literature: Nature and Scope', *Journal of the American Oriental Society* 101 (1981), pp. 49–86.

The *Aphorisms of the Philosophers* (*Nawādir al-falāsifah*) was composed by the physician Ḥunayn ibn Isḥāq (d. *c*. 873 CE), who was also the major translator into Arabic of Greek medical and philosophical writings. This text has been published as Ḥunayn ibn Isḥāq, *Adāb al-falāsifah* (*Sentences des philosophes*), ed. ʿAbd al-Raḥmān Badawī (Kuwait, 1985).

For Pythagoras, Ibn Abī Uṣaybiʿah specified al-Mubashshir ibn Fātik as his source. For Hippocrates,

Ibn Abī Uṣaybiʿah stated that al-Mubashshir ibn Fātik was the source for the sayings attributed to Hippocrates in section 4.1.8.4 of *Best Accounts of the Classes of Physicians*, while for those aphorisms given in section 4.1.8.2 the source is stated to be the *Aphorisms of the Philosophers* composed by the physician Ḥunayn ibn Isḥāq. However, for the majority of maxims attributed to Hippocrates by Ibn Abī Uṣaybiʿah no specific source is provided.

Choice Wise Sayings and Fine Statements by al-Mubashshir ibn Fātik is stated to be the source for all the aphorisms attributed to Socrates, Plato and Aristotle, as well as for some (those in section 5.1.35 of *Best Accounts of the Classes of Physicians* attributed to Galen). Ḥunayn ibn Isḥāq's *Aphorisms of the Philosophers* is the specified source for the sayings attributed to Galen in section 5.1.34 of *Best Accounts of the Classes of Physicians*.

For the vast majority of aphorisms attributed to the sixteen Arabic writers quoted in this book, no source is specified. For Ibn Abjar al-Kinānī (seventh–early eighth century CE), the source for the quotation is stated to be one 'Sufyān', which is probably a reference to the Ḥadīth scholar Sufyān ibn Saʿīd al-Thawrī, of the mid-eighth century.

Most of the aphorisms attributed to al-Kindī (d. *c.* 870 CE) were taken from *The Book of Prolegomena* (*Kitāb al-Muqaddimāt*) by Ibn Bakhtawayh, which was composed in 1029-1030 CE and also known as *Kitāb Kanz al-aṭibbāʾ*; two aphorisms, however, have no specified source.

For Ibn Riḍwān (d. *c.* 1061 CE), Ibn Abī Uṣaybiʿah states that he transcribed the sayings from a manuscript in Ibn Riḍwān's own handwriting.

In the case of Ibn al-Tilmīdh (d. 1165 CE), one aphorism (10.64.18 in *Best Accounts of the Classes of Physicians*) was related to Ibn Abī Uṣaybiʿah by a colleague of his who was a court physician in Damascus, Ibn Raqīqah (d. 1238 CE), who in turn heard it from the philosopher-physician Fakhr al-Dīn al-Māridinī (d. 1145 CE), who had been a student of Ibn al-Tilmīdh. The other aphorisms attributed to Ibn al-Tilmīdh were told to Ibn Abī Uṣaybiʿah by the poet al-Suṭayl (d. 1257 CE), who heard them from his father.

FURTHER
READING

For readers who wish to know more about these
aphorisms, or wish to see a complete Arabic version as
recorded by Ibn Abī Uṣaybiʿah, his history of physicians,
Best Accounts of the Classes of Physicians, has now been
published in full with an English translation as *A Literary
History of Medicine: The ʿUyūn al-anbāʾ fī ṭabaqāt al-aṭibbāʾ
of Ibn Abī Uṣaybiʿah*, edited and translated, with essays, by
Emilie Savage-Smith, Simon Swain and Geert Jan van
Gelder, with Ignacio Sánchez, N. Peter Joosse, Alasdair
Watson, Bruce Inksetter and Franak Hilloowala (Leiden:
Brill, 2020), in a five-volume print edition and also free
online at brill.com/view/db/lhom. The name of the
person to whom a saying is attributed can be easily
searched in the online version or found in the indexes to
the print version.

In addition, a new translation of selections from the biographies (but not the aphorisms) has recently been published in the Oxford World's Classics as Ibn Abī Uṣaybiʿah, *Anecdotes and Antidotes: A Medieval Arabic History of Physicians*, edited by Henrietta Sharp Cockrell, introduction by Geert Jan van Gelder (Oxford: Oxford University Press, 2020).

NOTES

EI2   *Encyclopaedia of Islam*, 2nd edition; available for subscribers at referenceworks.brillonline.com/browse/encyclopaedia-of-islam-2.

EI3   *Encyclopaedia of Islam*, 3rd edition; available for subscribers at referenceworks.brillonline.com/browse/encyclopaedia-of-islam-3.

ALHOM   Ibn Abī Uṣaybiʿah, *Best Accounts of the Classes of Physicians*, translated as *A Literary History of Medicine: The ʿUyūn al-anbāʾ fī ṭabaqāt al-aṭibbāʾ of Ibn Abī Uṣaybiʿah*, ed. Emilie Savage-Smith, Simon Swain and Geert Jan van Gelder et al. (Leiden: Brill, 2020).

OCD   *Oxford Classical Dictionary,* available for subscribers at www.oxfordreference.com.

SEP   *Stanford Encyclopedia of Philosophy*, available at plato.stanford.edu.

1. See E. Savage-Smith, *A New Catalogue of Arabic Manuscripts in the Bodleian Library, University of Oxford*, Volume I: *Medicine* (Oxford: Oxford University Press, 2011), pp. 446–61.

2. See *The Faber Book of Aphorisms*, ed. W.H. Auden and Louis Kronenberger (London: Faber & Faber, 1964). Ibn Abī Uṣaybiʿah would have approved of Auden's definition. See also 'Aphorism', *Oxford English Dictionary*; 'Aphorism' (Lutz Berger), *EI3*; Andrew Hui, 'Aphorism', *New Literary History* 50, 2019, pp. 417–21.

3. See, for example, Quentin Shaw, 'On Aphorisms', *British Journal of General Practice* 59, 2009, pp. 954–5; B. Campbell, 'Surgical Aphorisms', *British Journal of Surgery* 100, 2013, pp. 1673–4; and Richard I. Shader, 'Seven Aphorisms about Therapeutic Relationships and Listening', *Journal of Clinical Psychopharmacology* 39, 2019, pp. 95–6.

4. Ibn Abī Uṣaybiʿah devoted a long section (4.3) to Pythagoras in the fourth section of *ALHOM*. For the reception of Pythagoras in the Islamic world and his influence, see also 'Fīthāghūras' (F. Rosenthal), in *EI2*. For the ancient Greek and Roman world, see 'Pythagoras' (C. Huffman), in *SEP*.

5. The life and works of Hippocrates open the lengthy chapter on Greek physicians (section 4.1 of *ALHOM*). For the influence of Hippocrates in the Islamic world, see 'Hippocrates' (G. Strohmaier), in *EI3*; for the Greco-Roman world, 'Hippocrates (2) of Cos, physician' (J.T. Vallance), in *OCD*.

6. The life and works of Socrates occupy section 4.4 in the account of Greek physicians in *ALHOM*. For the role of

Socrates in Arabic literature and thought, see *EI2*, article 'Suḳraṭ' (R. Arnaldez); and I. Alon, *Socrates in Medieval Arabic Literature* (Leiden: Brill, 1991). See also *SEP*, entry 'Socrates' (D. Nails); 'Socrates' (A. Nehamas), in *OCD*.

7. The life and works of Plato are at section 4.5 in the long account of Greek physicians in *ALHOM*. See 'Aflaṭūn' (R. Walzer), in *EI2*; and A.S. Swift Riginos, *Platonica: The Anecdotes Concerning the Life and Writings of Plato* (Leiden: Brill, 1976). See also 'Plato' (R. Kraut), in *SEP*; and 'Plato (2) of Athens, *c.* 429–347' (J. Annas), in *OCD*.

8. The life and works of Aristotle occupy section 4.6, following the section on Plato, in *ALHOM*. See 'Aristotle and Aristotelianism' (C. D'Ancona), in *EI3*; 'Aristotle' (Ch. Shields), in *SEP*; and 'Aristotle (384–322 BC), philosopher' (M.C. Nussbaum and C. Osborne), in *OCD*. See also D. Gutas, 'Aristotle and the Early Peripatos: The Spurious and the Authentic in the Arabic Lives of Aristotle' in J. Kraye, W.F. Ryan and C.B. Schmitt, eds, *Pseudo-Aristotle in the Middle Ages: The Theology and Other Texts* (London: Warburg Institute, 1986), pp. 15–36.

9. The biography of Galen occupies most of the fifth section of *ALHOM*. See 'Galen' (V. Boudon-Millot), in *EI3*; 'Galen' (P.N. Singer), in *SEP*; and 'Galen, of Pergamum (AD 129–216)' (L. Edelstein and V. Nutton), in *OCD*.

10. His biography occupies section 7.1 of *ALHOM*. See 'al-Ḥārith b. Kalada' (B. Inksetter), in *EI3*.

11. His biography occupies section 7.9 of *ALHOM*.

12. His biography is given in section 7.4 of *ALHOM*.

13. His biography is given in section 8.4 of *ALHOM*. See also 'The Ibn Bukhtīshū Family' (B. Inksetter), in *EI3*.

14. His biography is given in section 11.4 of *ALHOM*. See also 'al-Ṭabarī' (D. Thomas), in *EI2*.

15. His biography is in section 8.26 of *ALHOM*. See also 'Ibn Māsawayh' (J.-C. Vadet), in *EI2*.

16. His biography is given in section 10.1 of *ALHOM*. See also 'al-Kindī' (P. Adamson), in *EI3*; and 'al-Kindī' (P. Adamson), in *SEP*.

17. His lengthy biography forms section 8.29 of *ALHOM*. See also 'Ḥunayn b. Isḥāḳ' (G. Strohmaier), in *EI3*. For the autobiographical portions, see D.F. Reynolds et al., *Interpreting the Self: Autobiography in the Arabic Literary Tradition* (Berkeley: University of California Press, 2001), pp. 107–18.

18. His biography is in section 10.3 of *ALHOM* . See also R. Rashed, *Thābit ibn Qurra: Science and Philosophy in Ninth-Century Baghdad* (Berlin: De Gruyter, 2009); 'Thābit b. Ḳurra' (R. Rashed and R. Morelon), in *EI2*; and 'Thābit ibn Qurra' (D. Reisman), in *Encyclopaedia of Medieval Philosophy*.

19. His biography is given in section 8.30 of *ALHOM* following the biography of his father, Ḥunayn ibn Isḥāq. See also 'Isḥāq b. Ḥunayn' (G. Strohmaier), in *EI3*.

20. His lengthy biography forms section 11.5 of *ALHOM*. See also 'al-Rāzī' (L.E. Goodman), in *EI2*; and 'Abu Bakr al-Razi' (P. Adamson), in *SEP*.

21. His biography is given in section 11.12 of *ALHOM*. See also 'Isā b. Yaḥyā l-Masiḥī al-Jurjānī (E. Savage-Smith), in *EI3*; and E. Savage-Smith, 'New Evidence for the Frankish Study of Arabic Medical Texts in the Crusader Period', *Crusades* 5 (2006), pp. 99–112.

22. His biography is given in section 11.9 of *ALHOM*. See 'Ebn
    Hendu' (L Richter-Bernberg), in *Encyclopaedia Iranica*;
    'Ibn Hindū' (H.H. Biesterfeldt), in *EI3*; and Ibn Hindū,
    *The Key to Medicine and a Guide for Students (Miftāḥ al-ṭibb
    wa-minhāj al-ṭullāb)*, trans. Aida Tibi with E. Savage-
    Smith (Reading: Great Books of Islamic Civilization,
    2010).

23. His biography is given at section 14.25 of *ALHOM*. See
    also J. Schacht and M. Meyerhof, *The Medico-Philosophical
    Controversy between Ibn Butlan of Baghdad and Ibn Ridwan
    of Cairo: A Contribution to the History of Greek Learning
    among the Arabs* (Cairo: Cairo University Press, 1937); and
    'Ibn Riḍwān' (J. Schacht), in *EI2*.

24. His biography is given in section 10.64 of *ALHOM*. See
    also 'Ibn al-Tilmīdh' (M. Meyerhof), in *EI2*.

25. His biography is given in section 10.69 of *ALHOM* . See
    also 'Ibn al-Ṣā'igh al-ʿAntarī' (G.J. van Gelder), in *EI3*.

ACKNOWLEDGEMENTS

Responsibility for the English translations of the
404 sayings or aphorisms drawn from Ibn Abī
Uṣaybiʿah's thirteenth-century universal history of
physicians has been shared by the eight editors and
translators of *A Literary History of Medicine: The ʿUyūn
al-anbāʾ fī ṭabaqāt al-aṭibbāʾ of Ibn Abī Uṣaybiʿah,* edited and
translated, with essays, by Emilie Savage-Smith, Simon
Swain and Geert Jan van Gelder, with Ignacio Sánchez,
N. Peter Joosse, Alasdair Watson, Bruce Inksetter and
Franak Hilloowala (Leiden: Brill, 2020). This publication
is available in a five-volume print edition and also free
online (with the generous support of the Wellcome
Trust) at brill.com/view/db/lhom.

The editors of the sayings for the present volume
wish also to thank Daniel Burt and Dr Selma Tibi Harb

for patiently looking over the order and arrangement of the aphorisms, as well as the anonymous reader for the press, who provided many thoughtful and helpful suggestions. In addition, the editors wish to acknowledge the help of Janice Venables and the other members of the watercolour & drawing class held at the Womens' Institute in Oxford under the guidance of the water-colourist Christina Wartke-Dunbar for their comments on the selection.

INDEX

Page numbers in italics refer to sayings attributed to that person